Mole and Frog

John Guthrie

Illustrated by
Angela K. James

For George, with much love.

The Garden

There was a lawn, with borders of colourful flowers in the Spring and Summer.

There was a vegetable patch.

There was a low wall, and beyond that was a raised area, in which everything else was. A little swampy pond, blackcurrant bushes, some other bushes with colourful flowers in the Spring and Summer.

After that, was the fence, and beyond, a lot of trees.

In the swampy pond lived a frog. Most of the time, he sat deep and safe in the water, with his large eyes poking out. With his large eyes, he could see all the usual things that frogs see from their ponds. But he could also see the entrance to the tunnel where the mole lived.

Most of the time, the mole was busy, or not busy, in his tunnel, where he felt safe.

But sometimes, the mole came out of his tunnel, and the frog came out of his pond, and they did things together, or they didn't do things together.

Being together was the important thing.

It's nice to be safe in your pond, or your tunnel, but everyone needs a friend.

Chapter One

The Game

One day, Mole said, "I know what we can do."

"What?" Frog said, quite happy not doing anything.

"Let's play hide and seek."

"All right," said Frog. "Who will hide first?"

"You," said Mole.

"Right. Count to ten." Frog began to hop away, but he glanced back.

Mole was standing staring at him.

Frog stopped. "Mole, you must look

away, or close your eyes. Otherwise, you'll see me hide."

"Oh, don't worry about that," Mole replied. "Moles can't see well. I shan't see you hide. I can't even see you where you are now."

"Then how," Frog asked, "are you going to find me?"

"I can scuttle and snuffle about until I find you or bump into you."

"That might take a long time."

"You could keep calling. Then I could follow the sound."

It didn't seem like a very good way to play hide and seek, but Frog decided to take the easy way and agreed.

"Here I go, then. Count to ten, then come looking, or listening."

Frog wanted to make it as difficult as he could. He plunged through the hedge, through the thick trunks of the big bushes, and stopped at the top of the little wall.

Mole called, "Coming. Where are you?"

Frog tutted. This was *not* the way to play the game. It was going to be much too easy for Mole to find him. He called, "Over here," and stepped back.

Falling off the wall was very unpleasant. He hoped to land on soft soil.

Dong.

He had landed inside the old metal watering-can.

"This is awkward," he said to himself. "I can't jump straight up, and I can't climb."

He called, "Mole, Moley, Mole. Over here. Hurry."

"No, I shan't rush," Mole called back. "That would spoil the game."

"Mole! I have fallen in the watering-can."

"You've hidden in the watering-can? That's a good place. I don't even remember where it is."

"Underneath the bushes, underneath the wall. I fell in. I need your help."

There was a lot of rustling, and Frog saw Mole on the wall, looking down at him.

"I found you," Mole laughed. "That was a good place. My turn now."

"No, Mole. I fell in here, and I'm stuck. Fetch a stick."

Mole scurried off.

He soon returned and threw a twig down to Frog.

"What am I to do with that?" Frog asked.

"I don't know. I thought you had a plan."

Frog tried very hard to stay calm. "I do have a plan. I want you to find a big stick for me to climb up and out of here."

"Ah," said Mole. "Well, you should have told me that."

He scurried off again.

He soon returned, dragging a large stick. "It's a big one," he panted. "Here it comes. I'll just swing it round and ..."

Dong.

Frog turned to Mole and said, "Now we are both inside the watering-can, and the stick is outside."

Mole thought about it. "If you stand as tall as you can on your strong toes, I could climb up you, and with my strong claws, I could pull myself out, then pass the stick to you."

Frog couldn't think of anything better. He stood as tall as he could, and Mole climbed up him, and with his strong claws, and a lot of effort, pulled himself onto the top of the watering-can.

"I did it!" he called, raising his arms in triumph.

"Oh, dear," he said as he lost his balance and fell backwards.

Crack.

"Did you break anything?" Frog called anxiously.

"Just the stick," Mole replied.

He added quickly, "I'll go and find another one."

Frog waited patiently. It wasn't long before he heard Mole huffing and scuffling above.

"It's a thick one," called Mole. "Here it comes."

"Ow," said Frog as the stick hit him on the head.

But the important thing was that the stick was big enough. Very soon, Frog was out of the watering-can, very happy to be safely on the wall again.

"It's my turn to hide," said Mole.

"No," Frog replied. "It's your turn to think of another game. I've had quite enough of that one."

Chapter Two

The Pool

"Well," said Mole, "I mustn't sit here doing nothing all day."

"Why?" asked Frog.

"It's one of those things we say when we're enjoying ourselves and think that perhaps we shouldn't be."

"I don't," Frog replied.

Mole said, "Yes, but it's different for you. That is how you live. You sit under-water with just your eyes showing, you sit on a rock for a while, then you try sitting on another rock for a while, and that's your day done. We moles are busy. It's our way."

"That's fine," said Frog, "but this is your Frog and Mole time. It's a beautiful evening at the end of a very warm and sunny day. If you were underground, doing all that digging, you'd be missing it all. And we aren't doing nothing. Not at all. We're thinking, and discussing, and observing the world in all its ...."

From the other end of the garden

came the sounds of a parent and a little boy.

"Ah," said Frog. "It's the paddling pool problem. Young George goes in, then comes out. He walks about in his wet feet, then goes back in and makes the water dirty. Then, he comes out. Then, back in. Over and over."

"Restless," said Mole. "Busy like a mole."

"Restless because he finds the plain paddling pool rather dull. It's just water. Clear water. He wants it to be more than that."

"Hmm," said Mole. "What is happening now?"

"George has gone inside to play with his toys, and his mother has shut the door."

"Hmm," said Mole again.

Frog looked at him. He could see

that Mole was thinking, and it made him nervous.

"What are you thinking, Mole?"

"What? Oh, I was just, er …just, er … well, look at it from George's point of view. Would *you* be happy in your pond if it didn't have lilies, and flags and ferns, and all those other plants?"

"No," Frog replied. "It would be very dull."

"You might even leave your pond."

"Yes, of course, I'd … Mole, I hope you aren't thinking what I think you are thinking."

Mole was already nibbling at stems. "Just a few," he said between nibbles. "You won't even notice that they are missing."

"Mole," Frog said sternly, his voice very deep, his chest swelling. "I, I forbid this. It won't work. You'll be caught. They'll be angry. You must not meddle."

"Just a few more. Come on, Frog. Don't throw cold water on my plan." He stopped and laughed. "That was a good one. Did you hear what I said?"

"I heard. But this isn't a joking matter. You'll cause trouble. People don't like paddling pools to be filled with plants. They're called paddling pools because children paddle in them."

Mole stopped nibbling again. "Is anyone paddling in the pool? Is anyone happy with the pool as it is?"

"You are very stubborn," said Frog. He watched for a few more seconds, then said, "That will do, or I shall be the one with an empty pool."

"You're right," Mole said. "It would work better with some of the sludge that you have in your pond, but that might not be wanted in the paddling pool. This will do for a start."

"For a start," Frog repeated with a big sigh.

They gathered stems and flowers in their arms, and carried them to the paddling pool. Twice more, and the job was done, apart from a bit of arranging that Mole insisted on doing. He was studying what he had done, and trying to decide on further improvements, when Frog grabbed a paw and pulled him away.

The door was opening.

Mole and Frog crouched behind a nearby rock and waited anxiously for what would happen next.

"Oh, no," cried George's mother. "What's happened here? How did this happen?"

George laughed. "I don't know. But isn't it great?"

He leapt into the paddling pool and wriggled and squirmed amongst the plants. "I'm a fish," he cried. "A crocodile. An eel."

He sank under the water, with just his eyes poking out.

"Ooh, what are you now?" his mother asked, sharing his delight.

George raised his mouth out of the water to reply. "I'm a frog. Like the one in our pond." He made some frog noises, then lowered his head again.

His mother said, "Well, I don't know how it happened, but so long as you're happy, then I approve."

Mole and Frog scutttled back to their usual place, where a large grin slid slowly across Mole's face. "What do you think of my plan now?" he asked.

Frog grinned back. "I think it worked very well, Mole."

Chapter Three

The Friend

On Summer evenings, when the house had windows and doors open, Mole and Frog heard a lot of what went on in the house.

One evening, Frog said, "It's the dog again."

Mole nodded.

From the house, they heard the voices of different members of the family.

"She's knocked my drink over."

"Now she's walking on my

drawings."

"Move over. No, not there."

"Stand still. "

Bella was a clumsy dog. She sighed. *She* didn't think she was clumsy. Things were in her way. That wasn't her fault.

She decided to go outside. It was safer there. More space.

She went through the open door, turned to walk away and fell into the paddling pool.

Mole and Frog couldn't help laughing. They liked Bella. Whenever she saw them, she didn't chase them or bark. She sniffed them, and even licked them, before they hopped or scurried out of sight.

They felt sorry for her.

But when she rose from the paddling pool with a lily on her head, what could they do but laugh?

Bella heard them and sighed again.

She wandered along the garden.

Mole and Frog didn't even think of trying to hide. They sat in their usual place and watched her walking slowly towards them.

"Knocking things over again?" Frog asked.

Bella nodded. "I don't understand," she said. "They keep saying I'm clumsy. Do I look clumsy to you?"

She made a big sweep of her arm and knocked Frog into the pond and Mole off the rock.

"Oh. Sorry." She helped Frog out of the pond and sat him on the rock again. "I'd better keep still," she said and sat down.

Frog said patiently, "You need to think before you move. Look around you, and ...." He paused, frowned, and looked right and left.

"Where's Mole?" he said.

"Perhaps he's gone somewhere safe,"

Bella said.

"Mole!" called Frog.

He listened carefully to a squashed and wheezy sound which told him where Mole was.

"Mole is underneath you," he said. "You sat on him."

"Oh, dear. Oh, dear," said Bella. She stood and turned to help the struggling Mole.

Her tail swung round and knocked Frog into the pond.

"Oh, dear," she said, turning back to the pond and treading on Mole.

"Oof," said Mole. He had said that when Bella sat on him, but no-one heard.

Frog was always happy in water, but he wasn't keen on these unexpected plunges. He spluttered a little as Bella pulled him out again.

"So sorry," Bella said. She stepped back and stood on Mole again.

"Sorry. Oh, dear," she said. "Perhaps I am a little clumsy. I'd better go some-where else and stop bothering you.

"We want you to stay," said Frog. "Don't we, Mole?"

"Of course we do. You just need to practise moving around carefully."

"You really want me?" said Bella, her eyes wide.

"Yes, we really do," said Frog. "You are now our friend. Everyone needs a friend."

"Or two," added Mole.

Bella shone with happiness.

At that moment, George's father came into the garden. He called, "All right, Bella. You didn't have to go. We still want you with us, and George is missing you. Come back in."

Bella's happiness increased. "It's not that I want to leave you," she said. "But I'm a family dog, and I love my family. Do you understand?"

"Of course," said Mole and Frog together. "Visit us anytime."

"Oh, I shall," said Bella. "*They* are family, but *you* are friends."

She turned to run back.

This time, both Frog and Mole were knocked into the pond.

Bella didn't notice, and Mole and Frog didn't mind.